MAKE YOUR OWN
Jams and Jellies

First published in Great Britain in 2012 by Bounty Books,
a division of Octopus Publishing Group Ltd
Endeavour House,
189 Shaftesbury Avenue,
London WC2H 8JY
www.octopusbooks.co.uk

An Hachette UK Company
www.hachette.co.uk

Material previously appeared in:
All Colour Cookbook 200 Jams & Preserves published by
Hamlyn in 2012
Preserves published by Hamlyn in 2005
Pickles & Preserves published by Bounty Books in 2010

ISBN: 978-0-753723-90-6

A CIP catalogue record for this book is available from
the British Library

Printed and bound in China

Measurements: Both metric and imperial measurements are given
in all recipes. Use one set of measurements, not a mixture of both.

Standard level spoon measurements are used in all recipes
1 tablespoon = one 15 ml spoon
1 teaspoon = one 5 ml spoon

American cup conversions:

1 cup granulated/jam sugar	225g (8oz)
1 cup muscovado sugar	200g (7oz)
1 cup butter	225g (8oz)
1 stick butter	110g (4oz)

liquids:

¼ cup	60ml (2 fl oz)
½ cup	120ml (4 fl oz)
1 cup	240ml (8 fl oz)

The recipes in this book use an imperial pint (570ml/20 fl oz).
The American pint is 16 fl oz (480ml).

Yield: As a very rough guide, the finished jam or jelly will make
1½–2 times the amount of sugar used. The yields given for the
recipes in this book are approximate.

The recipes in this book have been developed and tested in a home
kitchen. Although every effort has been made to convey these recipes
as risk-free as possible, the publisher assumes no responsibility for
damages associated with the use of this book.

**In the US, there are certain guidelines for preserving and
canning set out by the food standards agency, USDA.
Refer to http://nchfp.uga.edu/publications/publications_
usda.html.**

Photographs © Octopus Publishing Group, apart from: pp. 18, 34
Bon Appetit/Alamy; p. 24 SoFood/Alamy; pp. 40, 50 Photocuisine/
Alamy; p. 55 Foodcollection.com/Alamy.

CONTENTS

INTRODUCTION

The preservation of summer fruits is no longer a necessity for our survival in the winter months. Yet there is still a great satisfaction in filling the storecupboard with traditional jams and jellies.

These wonderful storecupboard delicacies are made seasonally when fresh produce is at its best. The eating of them can also have seasonal associations: sweet delicate strawberry jam piled onto warm scones in the shade of a tree in midsummer, a chunky citrus marmalade spread on hot, buttered toast as an autumnal treat, or a tangy redcurrant jelly served with cold meats in winter.

Home preserving is not difficult and the recipes in this book are designed for simplicity and success, covering the basic traditional methods of making jams and jellies.

Utensils & equipment
There is no need to spend money on special preserving equipment as most kitchens are well equipped for jam and jelly preparation. The basic kit includes a measuring jug, kitchen scales, a good sharp knife, a long-handled wooden spoon and a large saucepan.

Heavy aluminium, stainless steel and good-quality enamel pans are ideal. Jams, jellies and marmalades need to boil rapidly, so make sure that the pan is deep enough to allow for this. A wide-topped preserving pan allows plenty of room for the evaporation of excess moisture.

A food processor, electric shredder or slicer will reduce the preparation time for some fruits.

A sugar thermometer provides the easiest and most accurate way of testing for setting. These vary in type and price, and many have clips which will attach to the side of the pan. Take your pick, but remember that the most basic is probably good enough if you only plan to make jam once or twice a year.

If you are making a jelly, it will need to be strained through a jelly bag or a large, clean tea towel and for some jams or marmalades a length of muslin may be required in which to tie up and boil the trimmings. Some jams have to be pressed through a

fine sieve and this should preferably be made of nylon.

When the preserve is ready for potting you will find that a small heatproof jug with a good spout is best for pouring. Special wide-necked funnels are available for filling pots but they are not essential. Save all your empty jars, wash them thoroughly and rinse them in plenty of boiling water before use. While jars with screw-top lids are a good idea, jams, marmalades and jellies may simply be covered with wax discs applied directly to the surface of the preserve to exclude all air, and the jars topped with pieces of cellophane secured with elastic bands.

When your preserve is finished and ready for storing away, label the pots neatly stating the name of your preserve and the date on which it was made. And with a little imagination, decorative labels, ribbons and pretty fabric covers can turn a simple pot of homemade jam or jelly into a welcome gift.

Jam-making basics

The following hints and tips explain the basics behind creating successful jams and jellies, so read them carefully before embarking on any of the recipes.

Preparing the fruit: For best results choose fruit that is not quite ripe, as it will contain the most pectin, without which the jam will not set. Fruit that is just ripe gives the best flavour and should still contain enough pectin, but over-ripe fruit should not be used as it does not make good jam or jelly.

Prepare the fruit according to its type, discarding any that is badly damaged or mouldy. Remove the peel, cores, stones, pips and stalks when making jam, but do not discard any of these trimmings – they often contain a valuable quantity of pectin and may also help to flavour the jam. Instead, add just enough water to cover the trimmings, then boil them for 30 minutes in a covered pan. Uncover the pan and continue cooking until most of the water has evaporated, then press the resulting pulp through a fine sieve. Add the extract to the fruit before cooking. Alternatively, if the fruit will need cooking for some time, the trimmings may be tied up in a piece of muslin or fine cotton and cooked with the fruit. After the fruit has cooled, the muslin

should be squeezed of all its juices, which are then returned to the pan.

Large fruit – for example apples, peaches or pears – should be sliced thickly; medium-sized fruit – such as apricots, dates and large strawberries – can be halved and the smaller fruits should be left whole. Kernels from the cracked stones of apricots and plums can be added to the fruit.

Softening the fruit: Choose a pan large enough to allow plenty of room for the fruit pulp to boil without boiling over. It is most important that the fruit is cooked until it is soft before the bulk of the sugar is added, as the addition of sugar has a hardening effect on most fruit.

Place the fruit in the pan with the water and about a quarter of the sugar (see the chart, page 9). Raspberries, strawberries and rhubarb require only enough water to moisten the pan, while the tougher fruits like apples, blackcurrants and quinces need

considerably more. Heat the mixture slowly to boiling point, stirring as little as possible, just enough to prevent the fruit from sticking to the pan, then cover the pan, reduce the heat and simmer until the fruit is soft. This can take anything from 2–3 minutes for soft fruits like strawberries, raspberries and blackberries to around 20–25 minutes for apples, blackcurrants and damsons.

To make a jelly, the cooked fruit has to be strained through a jelly bag or a large, clean tea towel. Place a large bowl on the seat of an upturned stool to catch the jelly and tie the four corners of the jelly bag or towel to the four legs of the stool just above the bowl. Alternatively, hang the bag from a coat-hanger

over the bowl placed on a shelf or ledge. Do not squeeze the bag at any time during the straining or the jelly will become cloudy. The fruit should be left to strain overnight to obtain the most extract.

Pectin: This is the substance present in fruit that makes the jam set when the correct amount of sugar is added and the fruit is boiled. Pectin is released from the fruit as it is cooked. Some fruits have a good pectin content: lemons, cooking apples and crab-apples, blackcurrants and Seville oranges; others, such as plums and raspberries, have a medium pectin content and many fruits contain little pectin – for example, strawberries, rhubarb and pears.

To test for pectin, take a teaspoonful of the unsweetened cooked fruit pulp and drop it into 2 tablespoons of methylated spirits. Shake well, then pour the mixture into another container. If, as you pour, you see that the fruit pulp has formed a few large clots, it contains plenty of pectin; if several small clots are formed only a soft set will result; but if many small clots pour out, the jam will not set and more pectin should be added. Cooked, sieved apple pulp can be stirred into the fruit at the beginning of the softening process, or lemon juice or commercial pectin stock added towards the end of cooking time. (Commercial pectin stock can be bought at most good supermarkets; follow the instructions on the packet carefully to obtain a good set.)

Acid: Acid helps to release the pectin from the cells of the fruit and is also needed therefore to set the jam. Lemon juice, again, is a good source of acid and should be added to those fruits that do not naturally contain a great deal of acid, such as apricots, blackberries, plums and strawberries.

Sugar: It is not generally essential to use preserving or jam sugar, which is more expensive than granulated, but it dissolves more quickly and causes less scum. However, for some recipes in this book you will need to use jam sugar with pectin. Add only the amount that the recipe states, as the proper sugar concentration is vital in obtaining a good set. Gradually stir the sugar into the softened fruit and heat slowly until it dissolves completely. Fruit with a good pectin content requires up to twice its own weight of sugar. If the sugar content of the jam is inadequate, the natural yeast may cause the stored jam to ferment.

Boiling: Once the sugar has dissolved the jam must be brought to a rapid, rolling boil. The rapid boiling must be maintained until setting point is reached – this can be anything from 5–20 minutes depending on the type, quality and water content of the fruit. Stir the jam at this stage as little as possible,

as over-stirring will mix the rising scum back into the jam.

Warming sugar: Always warm the sugar before adding it the hot fruit as adding cold sugar will make the temperature of the jam drop and, by the time it has risen again, the jam may be in danger of overcooking. To warm the sugar, tip it into a roasting tin and warm for 10 minutes in a preheated oven, 160–180°C (325–350°F), Gas Mark 3–4.

Testing for setting: Start testing after 3–5 minutes of boiling. Unless you are using a thermometer, remove the pan from the heat. Do not allow the jam to boil while you are testing or you may overcook it.

There are two main ways to test for setting – the thermometer test and the saucer test. Using a sugar thermometer to record the temperature of the boiling preserve is the most accurate. Hold the thermometer well into the jam but clear of the bottom of the pan. Most jams and jellies set at 104°C (220°F). For a double check, follow this with the saucer test. Place a spoonful of the jam on a cold saucer. In a few minutes the surface of the jam should develop an obvious skin if setting point has been reached. Push the cooling jam with your finger – if it is ready, the surface will form wrinkles like the skin of hot milk.

Skimming: Scum rises to the surface during cooking and this has to be removed before the preserve is potted. Use a slotted spoon to lift the scum off the surface of the jam, jelly or marmalade. If the preserve is not a clear one (i.e. if it is not a jelly or perhaps a fine marmalade), then a little butter may be stirred in to disperse the scum.

Potting, covering and labelling: Pots must be thoroughly cleaned in hot, soapy water, rinsed and dried, then heated with boiling water or in a warm oven.

Hygiene is really important when preserving. Make sure jars, jam funnels and screw-top lids are all sterilized.

Immediately it is ready, the jam or jelly should be poured into the sterilized jars. You can use a clean, small, heatproof jug or a wide-necked funnel for filling the jars. Fill them up right to the brim and place a waxed disc, waxed side down, over the surface of the jam to exclude all air.

The pots can either be covered immediately with screw-top lids or allowed to cool completely and then covered with lids or pieces of cellophane, secured with elastic bands. Label the jars with the type of jam or jelly and the date on which it was made, then store them in a cool, dark place. Once opened jars should be kept in the fridge.

What went wrong?
Everyone has the occasional disaster with homemade jam, but there's no need to despair. If your jam has not set it could be for one of the following reasons:

Insufficient pectin: Certain types of over-ripe fruit may have too little pectin. If the preserve is not already over-boiled, add sieved cooked apple pulp (see table page 9) and boil hard before re-testing for setting.

Insufficient acid: Acid is needed to release the pectin from the fruit. If the fruit had little acid the pectin may still be trapped. Check the chart on page 9 to make sure you have added enough acid; if not, try adding lemon juice, citric or tartaric acid now and boil hard.

Inadequate boiling: You may not have boiled the preserve hard enough or long enough.

Patience is needed for this. Carry on boiling and testing if you think all the other requirements are there.

Over-boiling: This is disastrous. Overcooked jam will not set. You can tell if the jam has been overcooked by reading its temperature. If it is considerably higher than 104°C (220°F) then it has cooked too much. If you really are determined to get the preserve to set you can try adding more water and pectin, but it is not usually worth the effort as you may well end up with a jam that has an inferior flavour, colour and appearance. Better to cut your losses and use it as a sweet fruit sauce to serve with ice creams or puddings, to flavour creams and mousses or to add to a trifle. You can even mix runny jam with canned custard and whipped cream and freeze it to make a fruity ice cream!

Simple guide

The following simple table gives a brief overview of how to make a successful jam or jelly out of a number of different fruits, with the quantity of water and sugar you will need per 500 g (1 lb) of fruit, and the setting agent required, if any.

FRUIT	Water per 500 g (1 lb)	Sugar per 500 g (1 lb)	Pectin or acid needed
Apple	300 ml (½ pint)	350 g (12 oz)	juice of 1 lemon
Apricot	150 ml (¼ pint)	500 g (1 lb)	juice of ½ lemon
Blackberry	2 tablespoons	500 g (1 lb)	juice of 1 lemon
Blackcurrant	300 ml (½ pint)	575 g (1¼ lb)	none
Damson	150 ml (¼ pint)	500 g (1 lb)	juice of 1 lemon
Gooseberry	300 ml (½ pint)	500 g (1 lb)	juice of ½ lemon
Greengage	4 tablespoons	500 g (1 lb)	none
Loganberry	1–2 tablespoons	500 g (1 lb)	none
Plum	2–4 tablespoons	500 g (1 lb)	juice of ½ lemon
Quince	450 ml (¾ pint)	575 g (1¼ lb)	juice of 1 lemon
Raspberry	1–2 tablespoons	500 g (1 lb)	none
Rhubarb	2–4 tablespoons	500 g (1 lb)	apple pulp
Strawberry	2 tablespoons	350 g (12 oz)	juice of 1 lemon or apple pulp

Apple pulp: Apple pulp can be used as a setting agent for jams and jellies as apples contain a lot of pectin. Follow these instructions to make enough pulp to set a jam made from 1.5 kg (3 lb) of fruit. Rinse and roughly chop 500 g (1 lb) of cooking apples. Place the apples in a saucepan with 300 ml (½ pint) water, bring to the boil, then cook, covered, for 20–25 minutes, until they are reduced to a pulp. Press this pulp through a fine sieve before use.

STRAWBERRY JAM

prep time: 10 minutes   **cooking time:** 20–30 minutes   **makes:** 5–6 jars

1.5 kg (3 lb) strawberries, hulled, halved or quartered depending on size
juice of 1½ lemons
1.5 kg (3 lb) jam sugar with pectin
15 g (½ oz) butter (optional)

1 Add half the strawberries to a large pan and crush them roughly with a potato masher. Add the remaining strawberries and the lemon juice and heat gently for 15 minutes, until the fruit has softened.

2 Pour the sugar into the pan and heat gently, stirring from time to time, until dissolved. Bring to the boil, then boil rapidly until setting point is reached (5–15 minutes). Skim with a draining spoon or stir in butter, if needed.

3 Wait for 5 minutes before ladling the fruit into the jars to prevent the fruit from rising in the jar. Ladle into warm, dry jars, filling to the very top. Cover with waxed discs, waxed side down, and screw-top lids or with cellophane tops secured with elastic bands. Label and leave to cool.

Strawberry jam is always popular and is quick and easy to make in summer when strawberries are cheap and plentiful.

SPICED PLUM JAM

prep time: 25 minutes **cooking time:** 50–55 minutes **makes:** 4–5 jars

1.5 kg (3 lb) just-ripe plums,
   halved and stoned
grated rind and juice of
   1 orange
300 ml (½ pint) water
1 cinnamon stick, halved
1 teaspoon whole cloves
1.5 kg (3 lb) granulated sugar
15 g (½ oz) butter (optional)

*This jam is delicious in
sweet bread rolls or fresh
scones served with
whipped cream.*

1 Add the plums, orange rind
and juice and the water to a
large pan. Tie the cinnamon
stick and cloves in muslin, then
add to the pan. Cover and cook
gently for 30 minutes, until the
plums are softened.
2 Pour the sugar into the pan
and heat gently, stirring from
time to time, until dissolved.
Bring to the boil, then boil
rapidly until setting point is
reached (20–25 minutes).
Discard the bag of spices. Skim
the jam with a draining spoon
or stir in butter, if needed.

3 Ladle into warm, dry jars,
filling to the very top. Cover
with waxed discs, waxed side
down, and screw-top lids
or with cellophane tops secured
with elastic bands. Label and
leave to cool.

CHERRY CONSERVE

prep time: 15 minutes   cooking time: 1¼ hours   makes: 3–4 jars

---

1 kg (2 lb) sour cherries
   (Morello or Montmorency),
   pitted
1 kg (2 lb) granulated sugar
150 ml (¼ pint) brandy or
   orange liqueur (Cointreau,
   Curaçao)

1 Put the cherries into a large pan and add the sugar. Pour in the brandy or liqueur and cook over a low heat, stirring continuously, until the sugar has completely dissolved.
2 Bring the fruit to the boil, then lower the heat and simmer gently, uncovered, stirring occasionally, for about 1 hour until it is reduced to about two-thirds of its original volume.

3 Transfer the conserve to warm, dry jars. Cover with waxed discs, waxed side down, and screw-top lids or with cellophane tops secured with elastic bands. Label and leave to cool.

This delicious conserve is perfect as an accompaniment to a special dessert. Use it to top a creamy vanilla mousse or as a filling for a cake.

WINDFALL APPLE & CIDER JELLY

prep time: 25 minutes + straining   cooking time: 45–55 minutes   makes: 4 jars

2.5 kg (5 lb) windfall apples,
    weighed after cutting away
    any bruised areas
500 ml (17 fl oz) dry cider
900 ml (1½ pints) water
rind of 1 lemon
about 1 kg (2 lb) granulated
    sugar
15 g (½ oz) butter (optional)

1 Wash and roughly chop the apples, without peeling or coring first. Add to a large pan with the cider, the water and lemon rind. Bring to the boil, then cover and simmer gently for 30 minutes, stirring and mashing the fruit from time to time with a fork, until soft.
2 Allow to cool slightly, then pour into a jelly bag suspended over a large bowl and allow to drip for several hours.
3 Measure the clear liquid and pour back into the rinsed pan. Weigh 500 g (1 lb) sugar for every 600 ml (1 pint) of liquid, then pour into the pan. Heat gently, stirring from time to time, until the sugar has dissolved.

4 Bring to the boil, then boil rapidly until setting point is reached (15–25 minutes). Skim with a draining spoon or stir in butter if needed.
5 Ladle into warm, dry jars, filling to the very top. Cover with waxed discs, waxed side down, and screw-top lids or with cellophane tops secured with elastic bands. Label and leave to cool.

BLACKCURRANT & APPLE JAM

prep time: 25 minutes   cooking time: 50 minutes–1 hour   makes: 4–5 jars

---

1 kg (2 lb) apples
500 g (1 lb) blackcurrants
600 ml (1 pint) water
juice of 2 large lemons
1.5 kg (3 lb) granulated sugar
25 g (1 oz) butter

This jam is ideal as a filling for jam tarts or pile it lavishly in the base of a custard tart for a winning dessert.

1 Peel, core and slice the apples. Tie the trimmings up in a piece of muslin and place them in a large pan with the sliced apple, blackcurrants and water. Bring to the boil, cover the pan and cook gently, stirring occasionally, for 30 minutes or until the fruit is tender.
2 Allow to cool until the muslin is cool enough to handle, then squeeze out all the juice from the peelings into the pan. Add the lemon juice and sugar to the pan and heat gently to boiling point, stirring continuously until the sugar has dissolved.

3 Bring to a rolling boil and boil hard to setting point. Stir in the butter to disperse the scum and pot the jam in warm, dry jars. Cover the surface of the jam with waxed discs, waxed side down, and leave to cool. Top the cold jars with screw-top lids or with cellophane tops secured with elastic bands. Label and store.

PEACH & VANILLA CONSERVE

prep time: 20 minutes   cooking time: 25–30 minutes   makes: 3 jars

1 kg (2 lb) ripe peaches,
   halved, stoned and diced
1 kg (2 lb) jam sugar with
   pectin
juice of 1 large lemon
1 vanilla pod
15 g (½ oz) butter (optional)

1 Add the peaches, sugar and lemon juice to a large pan. Slit the vanilla pod lengthways, then scrape out the seeds and add to the pan. Cut the pod into very thin strips, and add this to the pan. Cook very gently, uncovered, for 20 minutes, until the peaches are tender and the sugar has dissolved to make a syrup, stirring from time to time.

2 Bring to the boil, then boil rapidly until setting point is reached (5–10 minutes). Skim with a draining spoon or stir in butter if needed.

3 Leave the conserve to stand for 5–10 minutes so that the fruit will not rise in the jars, then ladle into warm, dry jars, filling to the very top. Cover with waxed discs, waxed side down, and screw-top lids or with cellophane tops secured with elastic bands. Label and leave to cool.

RHUBARB, ORANGE & GINGER JAM

prep time: 10 minutes + cooling   cooking time: 1¾ hours   makes: 6–7 jars

1.5 kg (3 lb) trimmed
  rhubarb, sliced
50 g (2 oz) fresh root ginger,
  peeled and finely chopped
juice and chopped pared rind
  of 2 oranges
2 lemons, halved
1.2 litres (2 pints) water
1.75 kg (3½ lb) granulated
  sugar

1   Put two-thirds of the rhubarb into a large pan and mix in the ginger, orange rind and the juice from the lemons, then add the orange juice and water. Chop the lemon shells and tie them securely in a piece of clean muslin, then add to the pan. Bring the mixture to the boil, reduce the heat and simmer steadily, uncovered, for about 1 hour. The fruit should be reduced by half at the end of the simmering time.

2   Allow the fruit to cool, then remove the muslin and squeeze out all the juices from it into the pan. Add the remaining rhubarb, return the jam to the boil and simmer for 5–10 minutes, until the fruit is soft. Gradually stir in the sugar and continue stirring over a low heat until the sugar has completely dissolved. Bring the jam to the boil once more and boil hard to setting point. Remove the pan from the heat and, using a slotted spoon, carefully skim off any scum.

3   Transfer the jam to warm, dry jars. Cover with waxed discs, waxed side down, and screw-top lids or with cellophane tops secured with elastic bands. Label and leave to cool.

The ginger provides this jam with a real zing, which is wonderful with the orange and rhubarb. If you don't like ginger it may be omitted – the jam will be just as delicious.

APRICOT & DATE JAM

prep time: 30 minutes   **cooking time:** 50 minutes–1 hour   **makes:** 3–4 jars

---

1 kg (2 lb) fresh apricots
225 g (8 oz) fresh dates
600 ml (1 pint) water
grated rind of 1 orange
1.25 kg (2½ lb) sugar
25 g (1 oz) butter

1 Halve and stone the apricots. Crack the stones and take out the kernels. Place the fruit and their kernels in a large saucepan. Halve and stone the dates, removing and discarding their skins, and place them in the saucepan. Pour in the water, add the orange rind and bring to the boil. Reduce the heat and simmer the fruit, uncovered, for 30 minutes.

2 Add the sugar to the jam and stir it over a low heat until the sugar has completely dissolved. Bring to the boil and boil rapidly until setting point is reached. Add the butter to the pan, stirring it in to disperse the scum.

3 Pot the jam in warm, dry jars. Cover with waxed discs, waxed side down, and screw-top lids or with cellophane tops secured with elastic bands. Label and leave to cool.

Homemade apricot jam tastes superb, leaving the supermarket varieties in the shade.

BLOODY MARY JELLY

prep time: 30 minutes + straining   cooking time: about 1½ hours   makes: 4 jars

250 g (8 oz) red onions,
   roughly chopped
125 g (4 oz) sticks celery,
   roughly chopped
1 kg (2 lb) tomatoes, roughly
   chopped (not skinned or
   deseeded)
500 g (1 lb) windfall cooking
   apples, any bruised areas
   cut away, roughly chopped
   (not peeled or cored)
600 ml (1 pint) water
200 ml (7 fl oz) red wine
   vinegar
about 1.25 kg (2½ lb)
   granulated sugar
1 tablespoon tomato purée
juice of 2 lemons
15 g (½ oz) butter (optional)
50 g (2 oz) sunblush
   tomatoes in oil, drained
   and diced
4 tablespoons vodka (optional)

1 Add the onions, celery, tomatoes and apples to a large pan. Pour in the water and vinegar, then bring to the boil. Reduce the heat, cover and simmer gently for 1 hour, stirring and mashing from time to time with a fork, until the tomatoes and apples are pulpy.

2 Allow to cool slightly, pour into a jelly bag suspended over a large bowl and allow to drip for several hours.

3 Measure the clear liquid and then pour back into the rinsed pan. Weigh 500 g (1 lb) sugar for every 600 ml (1 pint) of liquid, then pour into the pan. Add the tomato purée and lemon juice and heat gently, stirring from time to time, until the sugar has dissolved.

4 Bring to the boil, then boil rapidly until setting point is reached (20–30 minutes).

5 Skim with a draining spoon or stir in butter if needed. Stir in the sun-blush tomatoes and vodka, if liked, and leave to stand for 15 minutes so that the tomatoes don't rise in the jelly when potted. Ladle into warm, dry jars, filling to the very top. Cover with waxed discs, waxed side down, and screw-top lids or with cellophane tops secured with elastic bands. Label and leave to cool.

This jelly goes well with cold meats, such as salami and Parma ham, olives and sunblush tomatoes.

DARK ORANGE & LEMON MARMALADE

prep time: 30 minutes + standing   cooking time: 2 hours   makes: 4–5 jars

2 large oranges, finely
  chopped and pips discarded
4 large lemons, finely chopped
  and pips discarded
1.8 litres (3 pints) water
1 kg (2 lb) granulated sugar
250 g (8 oz) muscovado sugar

1 Put the fruit into a large pan and add the water. Bring to the boil, reduce the heat and cover the pan. Simmer for 1½ hours.
2 Add all the sugar to the pan and cook over a low heat, stirring continuously, until the sugar has completely dissolved. Increase the heat and bring to a rolling boil, then boil hard to setting point. Using a slotted spoon, carefully skim off any scum, then leave the marmalade to stand for 15 minutes to allow the fruit to settle.
3 Stir the marmalade, then transfer to warm, dry jars. Cover with waxed discs, waxed side down and leave to cool. then leave to cool. Top the cold jars with screw-top lids or with cellophane tops secured with elastic bands. Label and store.

A small amount of muscovado sugar enriches this marmalade. For a tangy marmalade, use Seville oranges when they are in season.

BLUEBERRY & HONEY JAM

prep time: 10 minutes   cooking time: 20–25 minutes   makes: 3 assorted jars

600 g (1¼ lb) blueberries
150 ml (¼ pint) water
375 g (12 oz) jam sugar with
   pectin
125 g (4 oz) clear honey
juice of 1 lemon
15 g (½ oz) butter (optional)

1 Add the blueberries and the water to a large pan and cook gently for 10 minutes, until softened, crushing from time to time with a wooden spoon or potato masher.

2 Add the sugar, honey and lemon juice and heat gently, stirring from time to time, until dissolved. Bring to the boil, then boil rapidly until setting point is reached (10–15 minutes).

3 Skim with a draining spoon or stir in butter, if needed. Ladle into warm, dry jars, filling to the very top. Cover with waxed discs, waxed side down, and screw-top lids or with cellophane tops secured with elastic bands. Label and leave to cool.

A spoonful of this jam and a dollop of whipped cream make tasty additions to porridge.

30

ROSEHIP & APPLE JELLY

prep time: 30 minutes + straining   cooking time: 55 minutes–1¼ hours   makes: 4 assorted jars

400 g (13 oz) ripe red
  rosehips, left whole
1 kg (2 lb) cooking apples,
  roughly chopped (no need
  to peel or core)
1 litre (1¾ pints) water
about 875 g (1¾ lb)
  granulated sugar
juice of 1 lemon
15 g (½ oz) butter (optional)

1 Add the hips and apples to a large pan with the water. Bring to the boil, then cover and simmer gently for 45–60 minutes, stirring and mashing the fruit from time to time with a fork, until soft.

2 Leave to cool slightly, then pour into a jelly bag suspended over a large bowl and allow to drip for several hours.

3 Measure the clear liquid and pour back into the rinsed pan. Weigh 500 g (1 lb) sugar for every 600 ml (1 pint) of liquid, then pour into the pan. Add the lemon juice and heat gently, stirring from time to time, until the sugar has dissolved.

4 Bring to the boil, then boil rapidly until setting point is reached (10–15 minutes). Skim with a draining spoon or stir in butter if needed.

5 Ladle into warm, dry jars, filling to the very top. Cover with waxed discs, waxed side down, and screw-top lids or with cellophane tops secured with elastic bands. Label and leave to cool.

RASPBERRY & REDCURRANT JAM

prep time: 10 minutes   cooking time: 40–50 minutes   makes: 3–4 jars

500 g (1 lb) raspberries
500 g (1 lb) redcurrants
300 ml (½ pint) water
juice of 2 lemons
1 kg (2 lb) sugar
25 g (1 oz) butter

1 Mix the fruit in a large large pan and add the water. Bring to the boil, cover the pan and simmer for about 20–30 minutes, until the redcurrants are really tender.

2 Add the lemon juice and sugar and stir over a gentle heat until the sugar has dissolved completely. Bring to a rapid boil and boil hard to setting point. Stir in the butter and transfer to warm, dry jars.

3 Cover the surface of the jam with waxed discs, waxed sides down, and leave to cool. Top the cold jars with screw-top lids or with cellophane tops secured with elastic bands. Label and store.

This piquantly sharp jam can sometimes contain rather a lot of seeds. If you do not like too many seeds in jam, cook half the fruit separately and press it through a sieve before adding it to the remaining fruit.

ORCHARD FRUIT JAM

prep time: 25 minutes   cooking time: 40–45 minutes   makes: 5 jars

---

500 g (1 lb) plums, halved and stoned
500 g (1 lb) pears, quartered, cored, peeled and diced
500 g (1 lb) cooking apples, quartered, cored, peeled and diced
300 ml (½ pint) water
1.5 kg (3 lb) granulated sugar
15 g (½ oz) butter (optional)

1 Add the fruit to a large pan with the water. Cover and cook gently for 20 minutes, stirring from time to time, until the fruit is just beginning to soften.

2 Pour the sugar into the pan and heat gently, stirring from time to time, until dissolved. Bring to the boil, then boil rapidly until setting point is reached (20–25 minutes). Skim with a draining spoon or stir in butter if needed.

3 Ladle into warm, dry jars, filling to the very top. Cover with waxed discs, waxed side down, and screw-top lids or with cellophane tops secured with elastic bands. Label and leave to cool.

This jam can be used as a delicious filling between two shortbread biscuits, the top layer having a small heart shape cut out before baking.

PLUM & CRUSHED PEPPERCORN JELLY

prep time: 25 minutes + straining   cooking time: 40–50 minutes   makes: 7 jars

2 kg (4 lb) plums, left whole
1.2 litres (2 pints) water
about 1.25 kg (2½ lb)
    granulated sugar
2 teaspoons multi-coloured
    peppercorns, roughly
    crushed
2 teaspoons pink peppercorns,
    either dried or in brine,
    roughly crushed
15 g (½ oz) butter (optional)

1 Add the plums and the water to a large pan (there's no need to stone or slice the plums first). Bring to the boil, then cover and cook gently for 30 minutes, stirring and mashing the fruit from time to time with a fork, until soft.

2 Allow to cool slightly, then pour into a jelly bag suspended over a large bowl and allow to drip for several hours.

3 Measure the clear liquid and pour back into the rinsed pan. Weigh 500 g (1 lb) sugar for every 600 ml (1 pint) of liquid, then pour into the pan. Add the peppercorns and heat gently, stirring from time to time, until the sugar has dissolved.

4 Bring to the boil, then boil rapidly until setting point is reached (10–20 minutes). Skim with a draining spoon or stir in butter if needed. Allow to stand for 5 minutes so that the peppercorns don't float to the surface.

5 Ladle into warm, dry jars, filling to the very top. Cover with waxed discs, waxed side down, and screw-top lids or with cellophane tops secured with elastic bands. Label and leave to cool.

PEAR & DATE JAM

prep time: 30 minutes + straining & standing   cooking time: 1½ hours   makes: 4–5 jars

---

1 kg (2 lb) pears
500 g (1 lb) cooking apples
225 g (8 oz) fresh dates
900 ml (1½ pints) water
juice of 2 lemons
1.5 kg (3 lb) granulated sugar
15 g (½ oz) butter

This sets softly with a thick consistency – a jam for spreading in sandwiches with cream cheese or on slices of hot, buttered toast.

1 Peel, core and slice the pears, setting them aside, and place all the trimmings in a large pan. Rinse and dry the apples and chop them. Halve the dates, remove the stones and skin and place these trimmings in the pan with the pear trimmings. Add the chopped apples followed by the water and bring to the boil.

2 Cover and boil for 20–30 minutes, stirring occasionally, until the apples are reduced to a pulp.

3 Press the boiled mixture through a fine sieve into a large pan. Add the pear slices and date halves. Add the lemon juice and bring to the boil, then cover the pan, reduce the heat and simmer, stirring from time to time, for about 30 minutes, until the fruit is softened.

4 Add the sugar to the pan and stir the jam over a low heat until the sugar has completely dissolved. Bring to the boil and boil hard until setting point is reached. Stir in the butter and transfer the jam to warm, dry jars. Cover the surfaces with waxed discs, waxed sides down, and leave to cool. Top the cold jars with screw-top lids or with cellophane tops secured with elastic bands. Label and store.

note If you like spiced jam this is a good preserve to spice as the flavours of the fruit are accentuated and warmed by the addition of a cinnamon stick, a few cloves and about 2 tablespoons of grated fresh root ginger. Add these spices to the apples while they are boiling and continue as above.

THREE-FRUIT PROCESSOR MARMALADE

prep time: 30 minutes + straining & standing   **cooking time:** about 1¼ hours   **makes:** 4–5 jars

4 oranges
3 limes
2 lemons
1.5 litres (2½ pints) water
1.5 kg (3 lb) granulated sugar

If you would like to make marmalade, but are a little short of time, then this speedy fine-shred version uses a food processor to cut down on preparation time.

1 Thinly peel the rinds from the fruit, leaving the white pith behind. Put the rinds into a food processor and chop finely, then tip out on to a plate and reserve.

2 Quarter the fruits and process in two batches until roughly chopped, then put them into a large pan with the water. Cover the pan and bring to the boil, then reduce the heat and simmer for 45 minutes until the pith is soft.

3 Pour the mixture through a fine sieve into a bowl and leave to drip for 30 minutes. Press out any remaining juice from the pith with the back of a spoon, then pour the juice back into the pan and add the chopped fruit rinds. Cover and simmer gently for 15 minutes until tender.

4 Add the sugar to the pan and cook over a low heat, stirring continuously, until the sugar has completely dissolved. Increase the heat, bring to the boil and boil, uncovered, for 10–15 minutes, testing at 5-minute intervals until a set is reached. Using a slotted spoon, carefully skim off any scum, then leave the marmalade to stand for 15 minutes to allow the fruit to settle.

5 Stir well, then transfer to warm, dry jars. Cover the surfaces with waxed discs, waxed side down, then leave to cool. Top the cold jars with screw-top lids or with cellophane tops secured with elastic bands. Label and store.

REDCURRANT & LAVENDER JELLY

prep time: 25 minutes + straining   **cooking time:** 30–40 minutes   **makes:** 6 small jars

1.5 kg (3 lb) redcurrants
1 litre (1¾ pints) water
about 1 kg (2 lb) granulated
    sugar
15 g (½ oz) butter (optional)
8–10 dried lavender heads

1 Strip the redcurrants from their stalks with a fork and add to a large pan with the water. Bring to the boil, then cover and simmer gently for 20 minutes, stirring and mashing the fruit from time to time with a fork, until soft.

2 Leave to cool slightly, then pour into a jelly bag suspended over a large bowl and allow to drip for several hours.

3 Measure the clear liquid and pour back into the rinsed pan. Weigh 500 g (1 lb) sugar for every 600 ml (1 pint) of liquid, then pour into the pan. Heat gently, stirring from time to time, until the sugar has dissolved.

4 Bring to the boil, then boil rapidly until setting point is reached (10–20 minutes). Skim with a draining spoon or stir in butter if needed. Leave to cool for 5–10 minutes.

5 Ladle into warm, dry jars, filling to the very top. Cover with waxed discs, waxed side down, and screw-top lids or with cellophane tops secured with elastic bands. Label and leave to cool.

Pair this sumptuous jelly with scones or spoon onto a pavlova topped with fresh strawberries.

LIME MARMALADE

prep time: 30 minutes + standing   cooking time: 2¼ hours   makes: 4–5 jars

---

6 limes, washed, dried and
   quartered lengthways
2 lemons, washed, dried and
   quartered lengthways
1.5 litres (2½ pints) water
1.5 kg (3 lb) granulated sugar

1 Cut the lime quarters into long, very fine slices, removing all the pips. Cut the lemon quarters in the same way and mix both fruits in a large pan. Pour in the water and bring to the boil, then reduce the heat and cover the pan. Simmer for 1½ hours.

2 Add the sugar to the pan and cook over a low heat, stirring continuously, until the sugar has completely dissolved. Increase the heat and bring to the boil, then boil hard to setting point.

Using a slotted spoon, carefully skim off any scum, then leave the marmalade to stand for 15 minutes to allow the fruit to settle.

3 Stir well, then transfer to warm, dry jars. Cover the surfaces with waxed discs, waxed side down, then leave to cool. Top the cold jars with screw-top lids or with cellophane tops secured with elastic bands. Label and store.

This is a delicious and slightly tangy marmalade. Although limes are sometimes quite expensive, this recipe gives a high yield, which compensates for the initial cost of the fruit.

FRESH FIG & BLACKBERRY JAM

prep time: 20 minutes   cooking time: 35 minutes   makes: 4 jars

---

500 g (1 lb) blackberries
500 g (1 lb) figs (about 9),
    quartered
300 ml (½ pint) water
2 cinnamon sticks, halved
1 kg (2 lb) granulated sugar
juice of 1 lemon
15 g (½ oz) butter (optional)

1 Add the blackberries and figs to a large pan. Pour in the water, then add the cinnamon sticks. Bring to a simmer, then simmer, uncovered, for about 10 minutes, until the fruit is just beginning to soften.

2 Pour the sugar into the pan and add the lemon juice. Heat gently, stirring from time to time, until the sugar has dissolved. Bring to the boil, then boil rapidly until setting point is reached (about 25 minutes). Skim with a draining spoon or stir in butter if needed.

3 Ladle into warm, dry jars, filling to the very top and discarding the cinnamon sticks. Cover with waxed discs, waxed side down, and screw-top lids or with cellophane tops secured with elastic bands. Label and leave to cool.

Make the most of the flavours of late summer with this intensely fruity blend – ideal as a topping for natural yogurt or vanilla ice cream.

BLACKBERRY JELLY

prep time: 25 minutes + straining   **cooking time:** about 2 hours   **makes:** 5–6 jars

2.5 kg (5 lb) blackberries
3 lemons
600 ml (1 pint) water
about 1.5 kg (3 lb) granulated
  sugar

1 Pick over and rinse the blackberries. Place them in a large pan. Squeeze the juice from the lemons and add it to the pan. Chop the remainder of the lemons and stir them into the blackberries.

2 Pour in the water and bring to the boil. Reduce the heat, cover the pan and simmer the fruit for 1½ hours, until reduced to a pulp. Allow to cool, strain through a jelly bag overnight and measure the resulting extract.

3 Pour the extract into a large saucepan and add 500 g (1 lb) sugar for each 600 ml (1 pint). Heat slowly until the sugar has dissolved, stirring continuously, then bring to a rapid boil and boil hard to setting point.

4 Skim the surface of the jelly with a slotted spoon to remove all the scum and pour it into warm, dry jars. Cover the surfaces with waxed discs, waxed sides down, and leave to cool. Top the cold jars with screw-top lids or with cellophane tops secured with elastic bands. Label and store.

Here is a traditional jelly which is always worth the effort involved as it tastes delicious every time.

MINT & APPLE JELLY

prep time: 30 minutes + straining & standing   **cooking time:** 1½ hours   **makes:** makes 3–4 jars

2 kg (4 lb) cooking apples,
  roughly chopped
300 ml (½ pint) white vinegar
600 ml (1 pint) water
1.5 kg (3 lb) granulated sugar
125 g (4 oz) stalks of fresh
  mint

1 Put the apples into a large pan with the vinegar and water. Bring to the boil, then lower the heat and cover the pan. Simmer for 1 hour until the fruit is reduced to a pulp. Allow to cool slightly, then strain the mixture overnight through a jelly bag suspended over a large bowl.
2 The next day, pour the resulting juice into into a large pan and add the sugar. Cook over a low heat, stirring continuously, until the sugar has completely dissolved. Increase the heat and bring to a rapid boil, then boil hard to setting point.

3 Pick the leaves from the mint and chop them finely. Using a slotted spoon, carefully skim off any scum from the jelly, then stir in the mint. Leave to stand for 10 minutes, then stir well and transfer to warm, dry jars.
4 Cover the surfaces with waxed discs, waxed side down, then leave to cool. Top the cold jars with screw-top lids or with cellophane tops secured with elastic bands. Label and store.

This is a traditional way of preserving mint for use in the very early spring and winter months. You can also try using rosemary instead of mint, or a selection of mixed herbs. Serve with roast lamb.

REDCURRANT JELLY

prep time: 25 minutes + straining   **cooking time:** about 2 hours   **makes:** 3–4 jars

---

1 kg (2 lb) redcurrants
600 ml (1 pint) water
1 large lemon
about 1 kg (2 lb) granulated
   sugar

1 Trim any leaves off the redcurrants and place the fruit with all its stalks in a large pan. Pour in the water. Squeeze the juice from the lemon and add it to the pan. Chop the remainder of the lemon and put it in too.
2 Bring to the boil, cover the pan and reduce the heat. Simmer the fruit for 1½ hours, until it is very pulpy. Allow to cool slightly before straining it through a jelly bag, preferably overnight.

3 Measure the extract and allow 500 g (1 lb) sugar to each 600 ml (1 pint). Pour the liquid into a clean pan and add the measured sugar. Stirring continuously, heat gently until the sugar has dissolved completely, then bring to a rapid boil and boil hard to setting point.
4 Skim the surface of the jelly and pour it into warm, dry jars. Cover the surfaces with waxed discs, waxed side down, and leave to cool. Top with screw-top lids or with cellophane tops secured with elastic bands. Label and store.

This jelly is delicious spiced. Add a cinnamon stick and a few cloves, if liked, to the fruit as it is boiling.

CHERRY & RASPBERRY JAM

prep time 20 minutes **cooking time** 15–20 minutes **makes** 4–5 assorted jars

---

2 x 480 g (15¼ oz) packs
   frozen pitted cherries
340 g (12 oz) fresh raspberries
1 kg (2 lb) jam sugar with
   pectin
15 g (½ oz) butter (optional)

1 Add the frozen cherries and the raspberries to a large pan. Cover and cook gently for 10 minutes, stirring from time to time, until the juices run and the fruit begins to soften.

2 Pour the sugar into the pan and heat gently, stirring from time to time, until dissolved. Bring to the boil, then boil rapidly until setting point is reached (5–10 minutes). Skim with a draining spoon or stir in butter if needed.

3 Leave to cool for 10 minutes so that the cherries don't rise in the jars, then ladle into warm, dry jars, filling to the very top. Cover with waxed discs, waxed side down, and screw-top lids or with cellophane tops secured with elastic bands. Label and leave to cool.

This combination of easy-to-use frozen cherries and juicy fresh raspberries makes a rich, dark jam. You can use fresh cherries, if you prefer.

STRAWBERRY & RHUBARB JELLY

prep time: 25 minutes + straining   cooking time: about 1 hour   makes: 4 jars

1 kg (2 lb) strawberries,
  halved if large
500 g (1 lb) trimmed rhubarb,
  thickly sliced
1 litre (1¾ pints) water
about 875 g (1¾ lb)
  granulated sugar
juice of 2 lemons
15 g (½ oz) butter (optional)

1 Add the strawberries and rhubarb to a large pan, pour over the water to just cover the fruit, then bring to the boil. Cover and simmer gently for 30 minutes, stirring and mashing the fruit from time to time with a fork, until soft.

2 Allow to cool slightly, then pour into a jelly bag suspended over a large bowl and allow to drip for several hours.

3 Measure the clear liquid and then pour back into the rinsed pan. Weigh 500 g (1 lb) sugar for every 600 ml (1 pint) of liquid, then pour into the pan. Add the lemon juice, heat gently, stirring from to time, until the sugar has dissolved.

4 Bring to the boil, then boil rapidly until setting point is reached (20–30 minutes). Skim with a draining spoon or stir in butter if needed.

5 Ladle into warm, dry jars. Cover with waxed discs, waxed side down, and screw-top lids or with cellophane tops secured with elastic bands. Label and leave to cool.

CRANBERRY, APPLE & ORANGE JAM

prep time: 25 minutes   cooking time: 40–45 minutes   makes: 8 jars

2 x 300 g (10 oz) packs fresh
    or frozen cranberries
1.5 kg (3 lb) cooking apples,
    peeled, cored and diced
grated rind and juice of
    2 oranges, shells reserved
2 kg (4 lb) granulated sugar
15 g (½ oz) butter (optional)

1 Add the cranberries, apples and orange rind to a large pan, orange shells and any pips tied in muslin. Make the orange juice up to 300 ml (½ pint) with water then add to the pan. Cover and simmer gently for 30 minutes, stirring from time to time, until the fruit is tender.

2 Pour the sugar into the pan and heat gently, stirring from time to time, until dissolved. Bring to the boil, then boil rapidly until setting point is reached (10–15 minutes). Squeeze the muslin bag between two wooden spoons to extract as much juice as possible, then discard. Skim with a draining spoon or stir in the butter, if needed.

3 Ladle into warm, dry jars, filling to the very top. Cover with waxed discs, waxed side down, and screw-top lids or with cellophane tops secured with elastic bands. Label and leave to cool.

Try spreading cranberry, apple and orange jam liberally on buttered, toasted bagels.

MINTED BLACKBERRY & APPLE JELLY

prep time: 25 minutes + straining   cooking time: 40 minutes–1 hour   makes: 6 jars

2 kg (4 lb) cooking apples,
   roughly chopped (no need
   to peel or core)
500 g (1 lb) blackberries
1.2 litres (2 pints) water
1.5 kg (3 lb) granulated sugar
15 g (½ oz) butter (optional)
20 g (¾ oz) fresh mint, finely
   chopped

*This jelly makes a great
accompaniment for drop
scones and butter.*

1 Add the apples, blackberries
and the water to a large pan,
bring to the boil, then cover and
cook gently for 30–40 minutes,
stirring and mashing the fruit
from time to time with a fork,
until soft.

2 Leave to cool slightly, then
pour into a jelly bag suspended
over a large bowl and allow to
drip for several hours.

3 Measure the clear liquid and
pour back into the rinsed pan.
Weigh 500 g (1 lb) sugar for
every 600 ml (1 pint) of liquid,
then pour into the pan. Heat
gently, stirring from time to
time, until the sugar has
dissolved.

4 Bring to the boil, then boil
rapidly until setting point is
reached (10–20 minutes). Skim
with a draining spoon or stir in
butter if needed. Leave to cool
for 5–10 minutes, then stir in
the mint.

5 Ladle into warm, dry jars.
If the mint begins to float, leave
to cool for 5–10 minutes more,
then stir very gently with a
teaspoon to redistribute the mint.
Cover with waxed discs, waxed
side down, and screw-top lids
or with cellophane tops secured
with elastic bands. Label and
leave to cool.

INDEX